Diseases and Disorders of Youth

Kids and Diabetes

Toney Allman

ReferencePoint Press®

San Diego, CA

© 2019 ReferencePoint Press, Inc.
Printed in the United States

For more information, contact:
ReferencePoint Press, Inc.
PO Box 27779
San Diego, CA 92198
www.ReferencePointPress.com

LIBRARY OF CONGRESS CATALOGING-IN-PUBLICATION DATA

Name: Allman, Toney, author
Title: Kids and Diabetes/by Toney Allman.
Description: San Diego, CA: ReferencePoint Press, Inc., 2019. | Series: Diseases and Disorders of Youth | Audience: Grade 9 to 12. | Includes bibliographical references and index.
Identifiers: LCCN 2018010445 (print) | LCCN 2018011038 (ebook) | ISBN 9781682824009 (eBook) | ISBN 9781682823996 (hardback)
Subjects: LCSH: Diabetes in children—Juvenile literature. | Diabetic children—Juvenile literature. | Diabetes in children—Treatment—Juvenile literature. | Diabetes in children—Prevention—Juvenile literature. | Diabetes— miscellaneous.
Classification: LCC RJ420.D5 (ebook) | LCC RJ420.D5 A46 2019 (print) | DDC 618.92/462—dc23
LC record available at https://lccn.loc.gov/2018010445

Contents

A Miraculous Success

lizabeth Hughes was eleven years old when she was diagnosed with diabetes. The year was 1919, and although the medical community knew a great deal about the symptoms and outcome of diabetes, no one could save the girl's life. Elizabeth was a child of privilege. She was the beloved daughter of the well-to-do and respected politician and statesman Charles Evans Hughes. He had been the governor of New York, a Supreme Court justice, a presidential candidate, and the secretary of state. Elizabeth's father and mother had the influence and money to provide their daughter with almost anything, but they could not give her health.

Elizabeth's illness had a rapid onset. Suddenly, seemingly overnight, she became ravenously hungry and yet lost weight alarmingly. She was desperately thirsty and could drink quarts of water a day. She urinated excessively. She was weak and exhausted. Her parents took Elizabeth to the best diabetes doctor in the country, but there was little he could do. At that time, doctors knew that people with diabetes could not process food. They knew that such people had extreme levels of sugar, or glucose, in their blood and urine. They knew that some unidentified substance needed to process food was lacking within the organ known as the pancreas. And they knew diabetes was a death sentence. Elizabeth's doctor, Frederick Allen, had developed a treatment plan designed to reduce the glucose in the body by putting the patient on a starvation diet. With little or no food being digested, glucose was not produced, and life could be prolonged. Without the starvation diet, Elizabeth would be dead within a year. With it, she might live two or three years longer.

Elizabeth was already underweight at just 75 pounds (34 kg) and almost 5 feet (152 cm) tall, but she was nonetheless put on a starvation diet. The treatment was harsh and difficult. Some days Elizabeth was allowed no food at all. On other days she might receive some lettuce and a little bran and milk or meat. She was also allowed eggs and a few vegetables, after they had been boiled three different times to eliminate almost all the sugar and carbohydrates in them. Young people kept on this diet often died of starvation instead of diabetes, but Elizabeth stayed alive even though her weight continued to drop. By July 1922, however, when she was fourteen, she weighed just 45 pounds (20 kg) and was near death.

Then Elizabeth's mother, Antoinette Hughes, read a newspaper article that stunned her. Researchers at the University of Toronto had identified insulin as the substance that people with diabetes were missing in their pancreases. Already, injections of insulin had helped a young Canadian boy survive. The discoverers of insulin, Frederick Banting, Charles Best, and John Macleod, had figured out a way to purify insulin from crushed-up animal pancreases, and although their process was slow and crude, they were making enough to try it on a few patients. Elizabeth's parents begged for help for their daughter, and in August rushed her to Toronto for treatment. Banting began treating her with insulin injections twice a day. Within a week, the glucose in her blood was normal, and she was eating more than 1,200 calories a day. By the next week, she was consuming more than 2,000 calories a day, including foods she had not been allowed for years, such as bread and potatoes. She gained weight rapidly. From the Toronto hospital where she was being treated, Elizabeth wrote to her mother, "To think that I'll be leading a normal, healthy existence is beyond all comprehension. It is simply too wonderful for words."[1]

By November Elizabeth was back at home, strong and happy. She simply needed two insulin shots a day to manage her diabetes. She was the first American treated with insulin, but she was not the last. Historians estimate that she was one of hundreds of people pulled from the brink of death by the discovery of insulin in that first year. In the early years, insulin seemed like a miracle cure. In 1923 the *Toronto Daily Star* referred to its discovery as a "fairy tale of science," reporting that of "310 treated; 310 responded."[2] People who were expected to die regained their health instead.

Insulin, however, is a lifelong medical treatment, not a cure, and it is not even the best treatment for all people. As medicine progressed and people lived with diabetes rather than dying of it, doctors learned how complex diabetes actually is. It is not even a single disease. Elizabeth Hughes, for example, had type 1 diabetes, so her pancreas produced no insulin. Other people have type 2 diabetes and still make insulin, although their bodies do not use it correctly. Both types of this chronic disease require different and lifelong interventions. Even in modern times, research is ongoing to determine the best treatments. Researchers work to understand what is happening inside the body, why it is happening, what the long-term consequences of the disease and its treatments are, and whether a cure is ultimately possible.

"It is simply too wonderful for words."[1]

—Elizabeth Hughes, first diabetic in the United States treated with insulin

This research is important. Thirty million people in the United States have diabetes, and the numbers are increasing. Globally, the estimate is 371 million people. During 2017, according to the Centers for Disease Control and Prevention (CDC), the cost of diabetes to American society was $245 billion. This number in-

A young woman with type 1 diabetes gives herself an insulin shot. In the United States more than 200,000 youths under the age of twenty live with the disease.

cludes the cost of medical care and the cost of lost work and wages due to the disease. In addition, for adults, the risk of early death is 50 percent higher in people with diabetes than in people without it. Most people with diabetes are adults, but about 208,000 people living with diabetes are youths under the age of twenty. If these young people are to live long, healthy lives, they must be diagnosed early, treated effectively, and protected from the complications diabetes can cause as they grow older. Someday, the medical world hopes to see them cured.

Chapter 1

What Is Diabetes?

iabetes is a disorder of carbohydrate metabolism—the complex process by which the body turns starchy and sugary foods into energy. Several types of diabetes have been identified, but the major forms that affect young people are type 1 diabetes and type 2 diabetes. In all types of diabetes, the body cannot make or effectively use the hormone known as insulin. A hormone is a chemical made by one part of the body to be used in the functioning of another part. The insulin produced in the pancreas regulates many metabolic processes. It enables the body to use the fuel in food that is eaten to power the body's cells. Insulin is critical to maintaining life. The website Diabetes.co.uk explains, "The metabolism of people with diabetes is almost identical to the metabolism of people without diabetes. The only difference is the volume and/or effectiveness of the insulin produced by the body."[3]

Food to Energy

When food is eaten, the body digests or processes it using fluids such as acids, along with enzymes, which are proteins that catalyze chemical reactions. In the mouth, when the food is chewed, enzymes in saliva begin the process. In the stomach, enzymes and acid turn the food into a liquid mass called chyme that is pushed into the small intestine. Carbohydrates (starches and sugars) are usually broken down first and leave the stomach quickly; proteins and fats take longer to be liquefied enough to move on. In the small intestine, enzymes and other chemical substances break the food down into various nutrients. The enzymes come from the small intestine itself, the pancreas, the liver, and the gallbladder. Carbohydrates are broken down into the sugar known as glucose. Glucose is then absorbed through the membranes of the small intestine and subsequently released into the bloodstream, where it can be transported throughout the body.

Although body cells can get energy from proteins and fats, the glucose from carbohydrates is very important because glucose can supply energy very quickly and because the brain and nervous system need a continuous supply of glucose to work normally. Every cell in the body uses glucose for food and energy. Each cell is a complex little factory enclosed in a membrane. Cells in the heart beat; cells in the eyes gather light; cells in the lungs breathe. Every cell performs its special work in the body, and every cell requires glucose as fuel to do its job.

The Role of the Pancreas

The pancreas is an important part of this digestive process. In fact, it is considered to be a digestive organ. Fish-shaped and about the size of a hand, the pancreas is seated behind the stomach. It has two main functions. It produces and releases enzymes that digest fats, proteins, and carbohydrates in the small intestine, and it also produces hormones. The pancreas contains structures known as the islets of Langerhans (named for their discoverer). The islets are clusters of cells, and there are about 1 million of them, all producing hormones that help regulate the digestive system and the amount of glucose in the bloodstream. Islets of Langerhans have four main types of cells: Alpha cells

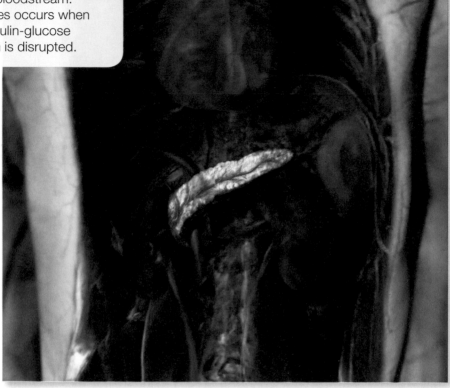

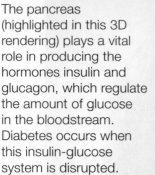

produce the hormone glucagon, which increases glucose in the blood. Beta cells produce insulin, which decreases the amount of glucose in the blood. Delta cells produce a hormone to help regulate the action of alpha and beta cells. And gamma cells produce a hormone that helps regulate all the activities in the pancreas.

Alpha and beta cells are the primary cell types, and glucagon and insulin work together to maintain an appropriate level of glucose in the blood. As an example, when a person eats a baked potato, which is high in carbohydrates, those carbohydrates are digested, broken down into glucose, and released into the bloodstream. Glucose in the blood rises rapidly as a result, and in response, the beta cells in the pancreas produce insulin.

The insulin enables the body's cells to use the glucose, and the glucose level in the blood drops. Conversely, when that same person goes to bed and sleeps all night without eating or digesting anything, the glucose in the bloodstream drops. If the alpha cells receive chemical signals that glucose is too low, glucagon is released. Glucagon signals the liver to release glucose stored there, and the glucose in the blood rises.

Without the pancreatic hormones, glucose in the blood would not stay in balance, but more importantly, the cells in the body would have no fuel for energy. This is because cells cannot use glucose without insulin. A cell's membrane acts as a barrier that prevents glucose from entering the cell, but insulin attaches to the cell membrane and signals the cell to absorb the glucose. Marcia Frank and Denis Daneman of the London Health Sciences Centre in Canada explain: "How does insulin work? It acts as a key opening the door to the body's cells, allowing glucose to enter and to be used to make energy."[4] Normally, insulin keeps the amount of glucose in the blood in perfect balance and ensures that the cells receive just the right amount of glucose needed for fuel. In all types of diabetes, however, the insulin-glucose system is disrupted. Glucose in the

> "How does insulin work? It acts as a key opening the door to the body's cells."[4]
>
> —Marcia Frank and Denis Daneman, diabetes experts

blood rises because it is not entering the cells, and it stays too high all the time. This condition is called hyperglycemia. In addition, the cells are not receiving enough energy to survive and function. Why this disruption occurs depends on the type of diabetes.

What Is Type 1 Diabetes?

Type 1 diabetes is a condition in which very little or no insulin is produced in the pancreas because most or all of the beta cells are dead. It is the more severe form of diabetes. Without insulin, the body's cells cannot get glucose and are literally starving.

Type 1 diabetes is often referred to as "starvation in the midst of plenty"[5] because plentiful glucose is circulating in the blood, but the cells cannot use any of it. Hyperglycemia occurs, while cells cannot function because they lack fuel and energy. Although type 1 can sometimes develop in adults, most cases have a sudden onset in childhood or adolescence. Type 1 may be diagnosed at any age, from birth onward, but the peak incidence in young people occurs between the ages of ten and fourteen years. Typically, within a few weeks, the child or teen becomes very ill as his or her beta cells stop making insulin.

No matter what their age, most young people experience similar symptoms. Kelly, for example, was thirteen years old when she developed diabetes. She remembers, "I was ill for about a month before being admitted to the hospital. During that time I had painful headaches from being dehydrated and was constantly sleeping and drinking gallons of water."[6] Kelly was exhausted because her cells were not getting any energy, but her other symptoms were related to the excess glucose in her blood. Her kidneys were working hard to filter her blood and absorb the excess glucose, but they were overwhelmed by the high sugar levels. As a result, they excreted some of the glucose into her urine, taking fluid from the tissues along with it. This situation triggers the kidneys to produce more urine trying to get rid of the sugar, and even more fluid is lost. Therefore, the teen became thirstier and thirstier and drank even more water, triggering the kidneys to produce even more urine, which eventually led to dehydration. Dehydration is a harmful loss of body fluid that can cause headaches, nausea, and dizziness.

Other people report even worse symptoms. Losing glucose into the urine means losing calories. Combined with the glucose never reaching the cells, this can mean being constantly hungry, eating a lot as a result, and yet rapidly losing weight. Some young

> "I was ill for about a month before being admitted to the hospital."[6]
>
> —Kelly, describing the onset of her type 1 diabetes

Prevalence of Diabetes in the United States

About 23.1 million people of all ages were diagnosed with diabetes in the United States as of 2015 (the latest that information is available). That amounts to 7.2 percent of the youth and adult population. The table represents the estimated number (in millions) of adults eighteen years and older living with a diagnosis of diabetes. It also shows the estimated number (in thousands) of children and adolescents who have been diagnosed with diabetes. As the table shows, the percentage of people diagnosed with diabetes increases with age, reaching a peak in those sixty-five and older.

Estimated Number of Diagnosed Diabetes Among Adults Aged ≥18 Years, United States, 2015

Characteristic	Diagnosed Diabetes Number in Millions
Total	**23**
Age in years	
18–44	3
45–64	10.7
≥65	9.9
Sex	
Women	11.7
Men	11.3
	Percentage
Total	**9.3**
Age in years	
18–44	2.6
45–64	12.7
≥65	20.8
Sex	
Women	9.2
Men	9.4

Estimated Prevalence of Diagnosed Diabetes Among Children and Adolescents, United States, 2015

Characteristic	Number
Age in years	
<18	132,000
<20	193,000

Source: National Center for Chronic Disease Prevention and Health Promotion, "National Diabetes Statistics Report, 2017," Centers for Disease Control and Prevention. www.cdc.gov.

people report craving sweet foods; others have to go to the bathroom extremely frequently; and some suffer with blurred vision. The blurred vision is caused by high glucose levels that pull fluids from the lenses of the eyes, which makes them lose the ability to focus. Eventually, this condition can permanently damage the eyes. When a very young child develops diabetes, it can progress to a dangerous emergency because the child is unable to tell anyone about the symptoms of fatigue, thirst, and excessive urination. India, for instance, is a teenager who has lived with diabetes for as long as she can remember. She says, "I have had Type 1 Diabetes since my 2nd Birthday. I was diagnosed after falling into a coma at my party."[7]

Diabetes and hyperglycemia can damage many body organs and functions. Children like India may develop a serious complication known as diabetic ketoacidosis (DKA). When the body cannot access glucose for energy, it begins to break down fats instead. This process leads to the production of chemicals called

Measuring Average Glucose Control

A very important blood test for people with diabetes is the A1C test. It is a measure of how well blood glucose levels are managed over time. The testing is usually performed in a doctor's office and provides a snapshot of a person's average glucose levels over a period of three months. A1C is not affected by one high or low reading or one spike in glucose numbers after a high-carbohydrate meal. Therefore, it is a more accurate measure of how well an individual is controlling his or her diabetes. The A1C test measures the amount of glucose stuck to red blood cells. Since red blood cells live only three or four months before being replaced by the body, A1C is an accurate test of average glucose levels for three months. The test measures the percentage of red blood cells with glucose attached.

A normal A1C reading is 5.7 percent or lower. A1C at 6.5 percent or higher represents diabetes. In general, good control for a person with diabetes is below 7 percent. Doctors can estimate the average daily glucose levels from the A1C reading. For example, a 6 percent A1C translates into average glucose numbers of 126 mg/dL, and an A1C of 12 percent would equal an average glucose reading of 298 mg/dL (dangerously high).

ketones. The buildup of a large amount of ketones is toxic, or poisonous, and causes the body chemistry to become acidic. DKA can occur at any age if diabetes progresses unchecked, but one 2014 British study found it to be especially common in young children. When children two years old or younger were diagnosed with diabetes, the study determined that 80 percent of them had DKA. Often, medical professionals fail to think of testing for diabetes in children so young, and this oversight can cause serious illness and even death.

Blood Glucose Levels

Testing for diabetes involves a simple blood test that demonstrates whether glucose in the blood is abnormally high. Medical professionals have determined a range of normal glucose levels and a range of excessive levels. In the United States the amount of glucose in the blood is measured by how many milligrams of glucose are in a deciliter of blood (mg/dL). A normal amount of glucose for a person who has not eaten in several hours (fasting glucose level) averages between 70 and 100 mg/dL. After a meal, this number rarely rises above 140 mg/dL. People with diabetes have a fasting glucose level above 125 mg/dL, which may rise to more than 200 mg/dL after a meal.

The higher the blood glucose remains over time, the more danger there is of complications and damage. Type 1 diabetes can cause blood glucose levels to skyrocket. Brittnay DeClouette, for instance, was ten years old when she was diagnosed with diabetes. She remembers her doctor saying, "Your blood sugar was five hundred and twenty four. I'm sorry, but you have Type 1 diabetes."[8] DeClouette, like all other young people with type 1 diabetes, has the most severe form of diabetes. It is a chronic, life-long disease that can cause extreme hyperglycemia and serious complications and medical issues if not properly controlled. Fortunately, DeClouette was diagnosed early in the disease process, before her hyperglycemia became too severe. When hyperglycemia is not controlled, long-term complications—including damage to eyes, kidneys, the nervous system, blood vessels, and the heart—may result.

What Is Type 2 Diabetes?

Type 2 diabetes is the less severe form of diabetes, and it progresses more slowly. But it, too, can be dangerous if uncontrolled. In 2005, for example, Minnie Ortiz was twelve years old and getting very sick. She remembers, "I was throwing up, really thirsty all of the time and felt like I could sleep all day. I was constantly asking for sugary drinks and foods."[9] No one knew what was wrong with Ortiz, and she did not see a doctor about her symptoms. Then one day at home, she fell into a diabetic coma. She was rushed to the hospital, where doctors determined that her blood glucose level was 1,200 mg/dL: extremely high and life-threatening.

Most people with type 2 diabetes do not suffer such extreme glucose levels, but they do have hyperglycemia. The difference between type 1 and type 2 is that people with type 1 cannot make insulin, while people with type 2 cannot use it properly. This kind of diabetes involves insulin resistance. The beta cells of the pancreas produce insulin in response to the presence of glucose in the blood, but the cells resist the insulin. The insulin binds to the cell walls, but this key fails to completely unlock the cell's door. Dr. Jason Fung explains, "During the phenomenon of insulin resistance, we imagine that the lock and key no longer fit together very well. The key (insulin) only partially opens the lock (receptor) and not very easily. Glucose cannot pass through the gate normally, and as a result, less gets into the cell."[10]

> "During the phenomenon of insulin resistance, we imagine that the lock and key no longer fit together very well."[10]
>
> —Dr. Jason Fung

In cases of insulin resistance, some glucose gets inside the cell, but not enough. The amount of glucose in the blood rises. In response, the pancreas—sensing that glucose is too high—releases more insulin to try to balance glucose levels. Eventually, the pancreas is working overtime, secreting lots of insulin but never catching up. Hyperglycemia and type 2 diabetes are the result. As time passes, overworked beta cells become exhausted, are damaged, and may die. When this happens, the pancreas can no longer produce enough insulin to reduce the glucose in the blood much at all. More extreme hyperglycemia occurs, and if it continues, the person is vulnerable to the same symptoms, DKA, organ damage, and complications that are a risk in type 1 diabetes.

Diabetes in Young People

Most people diagnosed with diabetes under age twenty have type 1. And most people diagnosed with type 2 diabetes are adults. However, according to the CDC, some twenty thousand to twenty-five thousand youth in the United States ages ten to nineteen have type 2 diabetes. More than 80 percent of them are overweight or obese, even though most people who are overweight do not have diabetes. Weight is related to developing type 2 diabetes, as is ethnic background, for unknown reasons. People most likely to develop type 2 are Native American, Hispanic, Asian American, Pacific Islander, and African American. Caucasians are more likely to develop type 1 diabetes.

Unlike with type 1, many young people with type 2 were not particularly sick before they were diagnosed. Many did not experience the symptoms of increased thirst, excessive urination, or fatigue. Often, the condition is discovered during a routine medical examination when a doctor decides to check blood glucose levels. Nevertheless, this chronic disease puts these young people at risk, even though they have fewer symptoms. By the time

A Rare Kind of Diabetes

A very rare form of diabetes can occur in babies during the first six to twelve months of life. It is usually inherited from parents and occurs in one out of every four hundred thousand births in the United States. It is called neonatal diabetes mellitus (NDM). Infants with NDM do not produce enough insulin. Symptoms include frequent urination, rapid breathing, and dehydration. About half the time, NDM is a permanent condition that requires the same lifelong care as other forms of diabetes. In half the cases, however, the disease is transient or temporary. The infant gradually develops normal glucose levels and normal insulin production as he or she approaches the age of one year. These children can remain normal or may have their diabetes reappear later in life, often when they are teens.

they are twenty-one, more people with type 2 develop complications than do those with type 1. Type 2 in youth seems to be a more aggressive disease than it is in adults, so complications occur sooner. The CDC reported in 2017 that almost 20 percent of youth with type 2 develop signs of kidney disease in the first few years after diagnosis; 18 percent have some damage to nerves; and 9 percent have eye damage. By age twenty-one, people with type 2 are also more likely to have early signs of heart disease, such as high blood pressure, than are people with type 1.

Diabetes is a disease that can be destructive to every organ in the body. Without usable insulin, glucose levels in the blood cannot be controlled. At the same time, the glucose is not available to fuel the body's cells. People with type 1 get seriously ill very quickly. People with type 2 may not be critically ill immediately, but they face progressive damage as time passes. Those with type 1 may be too thin, while those with type 2 may be overweight, but the effects on the body are very much the same. With both types, complications from uncontrolled hyperglycemia threaten health and even life.

Chapter 2

What Causes Diabetes?

Scientists and medical researchers do not know all the causes of diabetes. Researchers continue to try to unravel the mystery behind the disease. Nevertheless, ongoing research suggests that although genes and the environment play a role in the development of both type 1 and type 2 diabetes, the actual mechanism by which the types develop is different.

Autoimmunity and Type 1

Type 1 diabetes is an autoimmune disorder, a disease in which the body's immune system mistakenly attacks its own tissues. The immune system is the way the body defends itself against outside invaders such as bacteria, viruses, and other microbes that can cause disease. It is a complex network of cells and organs that recognize, seek out, and destroy any germs or other infection that the immune system identifies as "nonself." (*Auto-* is Greek for "self.") All the body's cells carry protein markers on their surfaces that enable immune system cells to recognize the cells as self. These markers are called antigens. Normally, all cells that carry the markers are left alone by immune system cells.

Cells of foreign invaders, such as disease-causing bacteria, also carry antigens on their surfaces, but these antigens are slightly different proteins, so immune system cells immediately recognize them as nonself. The several kinds of white blood cells of the immune system that circulate in the bloodstream spring into action. White blood cells known as B cells produce antibodies, proteins that attach to the antigens on the foreigner's surface to mark the invader for destruction. Other white blood cells, such as killer T cells, attack and destroy the infecting cells. The T cells attack only cells with the specific antigen on their surfaces to which specific antibodies are attached.

In an autoimmune disease, the elegant immune system process of identification and attack goes awry. For unknown reasons, the antigens on the surfaces of certain cells in the body are not recognized as self. The immune system goes on the attack, producing antibodies to those antigens and killing those body tissues. The medical community has identified more than eighty autoimmune diseases, and type 1 diabetes is one of them. In type 1 diabetes, the immune system identifies the beta cells in the pancreas as foreign invaders. Antibodies are produced, and the beta cells are killed. This process can take several years to occur, because the attack takes time. People do not develop symptoms until the majority of the cells are dead and unable to produce insulin. About 80 percent to 90 percent of the beta cells must be destroyed before hyperglycemia develops and diabetes can be diagnosed.

Genes and the Immune System

Why the immune system attacks beta cells and what triggers the action are questions that researchers continue to explore. Genetic factors, however, are known to play a large role in whether an individual is susceptible to type 1 diabetes. Genes are discrete segments of deoxyribonucleic acid (DNA) that carry the coded instructions that determine how cells function. They are the basic units of heredity and are inherited from the parents. Humans have about twenty thousand genes, grouped into twenty-three pairs of chromosomes in the nucleus in the center of each cell. Genes determine many individual traits and characteristics, such as gender, facial appearance, height, hair color, and basic temperament, like energy level and attention span.

Most genes are the same for everyone, but variations in genes are common. People have variations in eye color, for example, because of the gene variants they inherit. Blood types are determined by genetic variations as well. The genes determine whether a person's red blood cells carry the antigen dubbed A on their surfaces (type A) or the antigen B (type B) or neither (type O). People also can be type AB because they carry both antigens on their red blood cells. Variations in genes are normal and are called alleles. The three alleles of the ABO gene determine a person's blood type. Sometimes genes can also carry mistakes in their instructions that are similar to typographical errors. These errors are called mutations. Most gene mutations do no harm, but they can sometimes lead to disease. Some variations, too, can increase a person's susceptibility to diseases.

> "Inheriting certain versions (alleles) of the HLA genes increases the probability that immune cells will attack the body's healthy cells."[11]
>
> —Laura Dean and Johanna McEntyre, diabetes experts

Scientists believe that variations in genes make some people susceptible to type 1 diabetes. Chromosome 6 contains a complex of more than two hundred genes known as HLA genes. HLA genes carry codes that instruct the immune system's ability to distinguish antigens as self or nonself. Diabetes experts Laura Dean and Johanna McEntyre explain that "inheriting certain versions (alleles) of the HLA genes increases the probability that immune cells will attack the body's healthy cells."[11] People without these variations do not develop type 1. However, from 90 percent to 95 percent of children and teens with type 1 have at least one HLA allele known to increase susceptibility to type 1 diabetes.

Nevertheless, one HLA allele alone cannot cause a person to develop diabetes. Most people who have the variations never develop type 1. About forty other genes besides HLA genes have also been identified as increasing the risk of developing type 1 diabetes, including genes that code for making insulin and others that code for immune system functioning on different chromosomes than HLA genes. Multiple genes must be involved before diabetes develops, but scientists do not yet know how these genes work together to cause the disease.

Type 1 diabetes can run in families because genes and their alleles are inherited from one's parents, but the risk is not extremely high. Hayley, a teen with diabetes, says, "My mum has Type 1 diabetes since I don't know when so [I] always had a 50/50 chance of it being passed on."[12] Hayley may have had a 50 percent chance of inheriting her mother's alleles, but her risk of developing diabetes was only about 4 percent. If her father had been the one with diabetes, Hayley's risk of developing the disease would have been about 10 percent—the same as if one of her siblings had diabetes. If she had an identical twin—who shared the same genes—with diabetes, then her risk would rise to 50 percent. Researchers cannot explain these differences in inheritance, but they do know that genetics cannot be the only cause of diabetes. If it were, identical twins, for instance, with identical genes, would both always get type 1 diabetes. Genes are only a part of the story. Something must trigger the onset of the immune system's attack on beta cells, and researchers hypothesize that it is something in the environment.

Environmental Triggers and Type 1

One environmental factor considered by researchers is whether an individual is breast-fed as an infant. Some studies have suggested that babies who are breast-fed for several months are less likely to develop type 1 diabetes than those who were bottle fed, even when those babies carry a genetic risk. One theory is that early exposure to the cow's milk in formula stresses the immune system and may make it overreact to antigens of all sorts, including those on beta cells. The association is small, however; most bottle-fed babies do not develop diabetes, so other environmental factors probably play a role, too.

Another theory is that trauma to the body, such as a car accident or serious illness, may trigger type 1 in vulnerable young people. Any trauma puts a strain on the pancreas because any stress increases the body's need for fuel, energy, and therefore insulin. If an autoimmune reaction is already beginning in the body for genetic reasons, and the pancreas is not functioning correctly, the trauma might trigger the disease. Dr. James H. Warram of the Joslin Diabetes Center explains, "As the demands on the body increase, it can tip the body's insulin production system over the edge."[13] However, Warram is careful to say that trauma is not the cause of type 1 diabetes.

Hayley was diagnosed with type 1 after she was struck by a car. In 2014 scientist Rabie Karrouri reported on a ten-year-old boy from Libya traumatized when a mortar shell dropped near him during the revolution in that country. The boy was frozen in fear until his father rushed to him, scooped him up, and carried him to safety. A week later, after being brought to a field hospital, the child was found to have type 1 diabetes, even though he had had no symptoms before the trauma. Karrouri believes that the boy's type 1 was triggered by the severe psychological trauma. Other researchers have also reported cases of type 1 diabetes linked with "serious life events"[14] during childhood, such as a family death or divorce. Nevertheless, such events are only part of the possible complex causes of diabetes. Diabetes expert Dr. Richard Elliott explains, "It is important to note that, while instances of stress might coincide with or even contribute to a diabetes diagnosis, it is highly unlikely that such events would be the only cause."[15]

> "As the demands on the body increase, it can tip the body's insulin production system over the edge."[13]
>
> —Dr. James H. Warram

Many researchers strongly suspect that viral infections may trigger type 1 by activating an autoimmune attack. Whenever a virus invades the body, the immune system mounts an attack to destroy the threat and produces antibodies specific to the antigens of the virus. Scientists theorize that the antigens on the surfaces of some viruses are similar to the antigens on beta cells. This similarity causes an overactive immune system to mistakenly attack beta cells. Some research studies have found a link between certain viruses, especially the virus known as coxsackievirus B1, and type 1, but others have not. No one is sure what causes type 1 diabetes, and researchers continue to explore the combination of environmental triggers and the multiple genes that must be involved before type 1 can occur.

Type 2 and Environmental Triggers

Type 2 diabetes is also believed to involve multiple genes, but they are different genes than those involved in type 1. In addition, several risk factors have been clearly identified in its onset. More is known about type 2 in adults than in young people because many more adults have type 2 diabetes. Most researchers, however, believe the risk factors and genetics are the same, no matter what age type 2 develops. Some studies have been conducted with young people, and this research, too, suggests type 2 is very similar in adults and youth. Since type 2 is a disease of insulin resistance, the largest question to ask is what leads to insulin resistance in the first place.

Medical experts say that the single most important risk factor related to type 2 is being overweight or obese. According to the CDC, obesity is defined by the body mass index (BMI). BMI

A New Idea About Type 1

In 2017 an international research team proposed a new idea about the cause of type 1 diabetes. Dr. Bart Roep of the City of Hope National Medical Center in California led the American part of the study. He says, "Our findings show that type 1 diabetes results from a mistake of the beta cell, not a mistake of the immune system." This means that it is not the immune system that has gone awry and started an autoimmune attack on beta cells. It is the beta cells that are in error. The beta cells have faulty proteins on their surfaces, probably because the genes that code for the protein are mutated. So when the immune system attacks these proteins, it is doing the right thing. It is identifying and attacking malfunctioning cells to keep the body healthy. Roep's study is the first of its kind and will have to be replicated before scientists are sure of its accuracy. Nevertheless, the research team hopes that clearly understanding the cause of the autoimmune attack will someday lead to new therapies to prevent or correct damage to beta cells.

Quoted in City of Hope, "New Potential Cause of Type 1 Diabetes," ScienceDaily, March 1, 2017. www.sciencedaily.com.

Most medical experts agree that the risk of type 2 diabetes increases significantly in children and teens who are overweight or obese.

is a mathematical representation of a person's body fat in comparison to height. For young people, weight is also compared to that of other youth of the same age and gender, because percentages of muscles, fat, and bone weight vary as children and teens grow, and they are different for boys and girls. BMI growth charts have been developed to compare people at each age and gender. BMI is measured in kilograms of body weight compared to height in meters, using the mathematical formula. Where a person falls on the chart is measured in percentiles.

For example, 90 percent of children of a specific age would fall below the 90th percentile in a certain weight. Children and teens who fall between the 5th and 85th percentile are considered to be of normal weight. Those between the 85th and 95th percentile are considered overweight, and those at or above the 95th percentile are considered obese. The CDC says, "For example, a 10-year-old boy of average height (56 inches) who weighs 102 pounds would have a BMI of 22.9 kg/m^2. This would place the boy in the 95th percentile for BMI, and he would be considered as obese. This means that the child's BMI is greater than the BMI of 95% of 10-year-old boys."[16]

For adults, as BMI increases, the risk of type 2 diabetes increases, and medical scientists believe that the risk is similar for children and teens. Certainly, the risk of diabetes is known to increase in children and teens who are overweight. And children who are obese are more likely to be at greater risk of developing type 2 than obese adults. In the United States in 2017, about one in three young people were overweight or obese—triple the number who were overweight or obese in 1970. As the number of overweight youth has increased, the rate of type 2 diabetes has increased as well. Other risk factors related to diabetes and being overweight include physical inactivity and a diet high in sugary and fatty foods. In addition, extra fat carried around the midsection or abdomen seems to be riskier than fat more evenly distributed around the body.

Fatty tissue layers inside and between the muscles and skin around the abdomen increase the body's resistance to insulin. Insulin resistance causes beta cells to work to produce even more insulin until the overworked cells are exhausted, which leads to type 2 diabetes. At first glance, then, it would seem that being overweight causes type 2 diabetes, but this is far from the truth. Most overweight people—youth and adult—never develop diabetes. Being overweight or obese can be a trigger, but it cannot cause diabetes except in genetically vulnerable people.

Type 2 Diabetes in Youth of Different Ethnic Groups

Young people from certain ethnic groups are more likely to develop type 2 diabetes than others. The bar graph shows the incidence of type 2 diabetes in US youth, by ethnicity, in 2009 (the latest year for which data is available). Prevalence is reported as the number of individuals with youth onset type 2 diabetes per ten thousand people (ages ten to nineteen years). For example, fewer than two out of every ten thousand non-Hispanic white youth have type 2 diabetes.

Prevalence of Youth-Onset Type 2 Diabetes by Race/Ethnicity

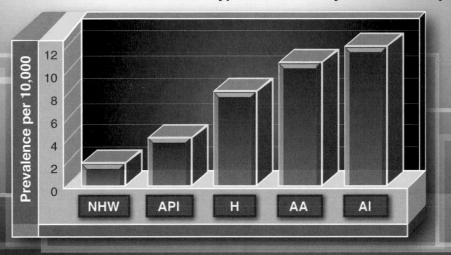

Note: Definitions: AA is African American; AI is American Indian; API is Asian Pacific Islander; H is Hispanic; NHW is non-Hispanic white.

Source: Kristen J. Nadeau et al., "Youth-Onset Type 2 Diabetes Consensus Report: Current Status, Challenges, and Priorities," *Diabetes Care*, American Diabetes Association, September 2016. http://care.diabetesjournals.org.

Genes and Type 2

Researchers have determined that the connection between genes and developing type 2 diabetes is even stronger than the connection for type 1. Type 2 diabetes runs strongly in families. Most young people who develop diabetes have someone in the family who has diabetes. Although some of this risk may be because everyone in the family shares the same food and exercise habits, some of the risk lies in their shared genes. One way scientists know this is by studying identical twins. If one twin has type 2, at least 75 percent of the time the other twin will develop the disease, too. When both parents have type 2, the chance that a child will develop diabetes is about 50 percent. In all families, if a person has a parent or sibling with type 2, he or she is five to ten times more likely to develop the disease than a person with no close relatives with type 2. Compared to the 5 percent to 6 percent increased risk for relatives of people with type 1, these statistics make it obvious that the genetic susceptibility to type 2 is high.

Scientists do not know which genes are responsible for susceptibility to type 2 diabetes, but in 2016 more than three hundred researchers in a European study of the genetics of type 2 reported that they had identified more than a dozen genes directly linked to developing type 2. Many other genes have been

Genes and Ethnic Groups

Human beings around the world share almost the same genetic makeup, but analysis of individual complete sets of genes (their genomes) demonstrates a few variations between different populations. That is why different ethnic groups may have different skin colors, height, or susceptibility to certain diseases. Emily Kennedy Anthes of the Massachusetts Institute of Technology explains, "Geography is linked to genetic variation, and people who have the same geographic ancestry are more likely, on average, to be genetically similar than people who do not." This is why, for example, African Americans may be more susceptible to type 2 diabetes, while people of European ancestry are more likely than other ethnic groups to get type 1 diabetes. This does not mean, however, that African Americans cannot get type 1 or Caucasians are safe from type 2. All genetic variations can appear in all ethnic groups because human genetic makeup is so similar. It does mean that some variations occur more commonly in some ethnic groups than others.

Emily Kennedy Anthes, "The Chosen Genes: Jews, Genetics, and the Future of Ethnic Medicine," DSpace@MIT, 2006. https://dspace.mit.edu.

previously identified as sometimes being associated with type 2 in some people. Scientists are not sure how these genes might interact with each other to cause type 2 to develop in people with environmental triggers. They do know, however, that many of these genes are responsible for how the body produces glucose, how insulin is regulated, and how the body senses glucose levels. They theorize that the more genetic variations that occur in multiple genes, the greater the likelihood that a person will develop type 2. The genes interact with the environment to produce the disease.

"Trying to understand the cause of diabetes is like peeling an onion."[17]

—David Mendosa, diabetes expert with type 2 diabetes

No Clear Answers

In both type 1 and type 2 diabetes, how genetics interact with the environment to produce the disease is still poorly understood. Diabetes expert and patient David Mendosa writes, "Trying to understand the cause of diabetes is like peeling an onion. Not only do both activities tend to make us cry, but also as soon as we reach one layer, there's another one to cut through."[17] Diabetes is such a complex disease that the medical world remains far from a complete understanding of its cause.

Chapter 3

Can Diabetes Be Treated or Cured?

egan Coleman has type 1 diabetes. The first thing the college student does every morning when she awakens is check her blood glucose levels. Coleman wears a continuous glucose monitor (CGM), which is a small device about the size of a pager. The CGM works with a sensor inserted just underneath the skin that takes glucose readings every few minutes and allows Coleman to check her status at a glance. If her glucose level is acceptable, she is able to get ready for the day and prepare breakfast. Before she eats, she counts the carbohydrates in the meal and gives herself an injection of insulin appropriate to that amount of carbs. Then Coleman heads off to classes. At lunchtime, she counts carbs again and injects another shot of insulin before eating. After an afternoon of water polo practice, the student athlete repeats the same careful carb counting/insulin injection procedure at dinner and also gives herself a shot of a different kind of insulin—long acting instead of short acting—to get her through the night.

At bedtime, Coleman checks her glucose levels again and hopes the glucose numbers stay in a good range throughout the night. She can never completely count on that happening, either at night or during daily activities. Sometimes her glucose level is too high, meaning she needs more insulin. Sometimes it is too low, meaning she had too much insulin and needs a sugary snack to make her glucose numbers rise. She says, "Luckily for me, my CGM will beep and wake me up if my number is too low or high in the night. But before we had a CGM, I (or usually my parents) would have to wake up every night, about two hours after going to bed, to make sure my number was in a good range."[18]

When the warning beep sounds, Coleman has to react quickly. She explains:

> If my number is high, then I will give myself a shot and set an alarm to wake up in about two hours to make sure my number has gone down. If my number is low, it might be a long night. If my number is only a little low I will eat something small, wait to make sure it gets into a good range, then go back to sleep, because I will be woken up again if it drops. If my number is very low, or it is dropping fast, I will have a bigger sugary snack, then either set an alarm for every 15 minutes to make sure it is coming up, or I will stay up waiting for it to come back up.[19]

Coleman admits, "Diabetes definitely has its difficulties."[20] Diabetes cannot be cured. Nevertheless, all kinds of diabetes can be treated, and most people who have it can live long, healthy, active lives. Treatment is all about management and control—control of glucose levels, control of insulin, and control of one's diet. Whether a young person is coping with type 1 or type 2, some treatments are similar, while others are specific to the type. And because each person is different, every treatment plan is adjusted to each individual's needs.

"Diabetes definitely has its difficulties."[20]

—Megan Coleman, who has type 1 diabetes

Type 1 Diabetes and Insulin Treatment

For type 1 diabetes, the major treatment is insulin replacement therapy so that the body cells can use glucose and hyperglycemia can be prevented. Insulin can be delivered to the body in different ways. Some young people, like Coleman, give themselves insulin injections, or shots, using a very thin needle or an insulin pen that automatically gives the shot when a button is pushed. The insulin is injected under the skin with the feeling of a small prick. (Insulin cannot be swallowed like a pill because the chemicals in the stomach would destroy it before it reached the bloodstream.)

Many young people avoid the need for shots with a device known as an insulin pump. The pump is about the size of a cell phone and is worn outside the body, usually at the abdomen. It carries a reservoir of insulin that is attached to a thin catheter that is inserted under the skin. The pump can be tucked in a pocket or carried on a waistband. It can automatically dispense small, steady doses of insulin in a way that mimics what a functioning pancreas would do. Such doses of insulin are called basal rates, and some research suggests that they control glucose levels better than periodic shots.

People with pumps still have to adjust their insulin injections when they eat a meal. At mealtime, they need an extra dose of insulin to cope with the carbohydrates that they are ingesting. But they can program their pumps to deliver the extra dose—called a bolus—every time they eat. Some pumps are combined with continuous glucose monitors. In this way, the device measures the amount of glucose in the blood and alerts the user when more or less insulin is needed. Blood glucose levels are continually monitored, and insulin is delivered without the need for repeated testing and needle pricks.

Many children and teens love these insulin pumps. Julieta Marquez, for example, received her insulin pump with monitor when she was seventeen. Before that, the teen had to do her own testing and injections. Blood glucose testing traditionally involves pricking

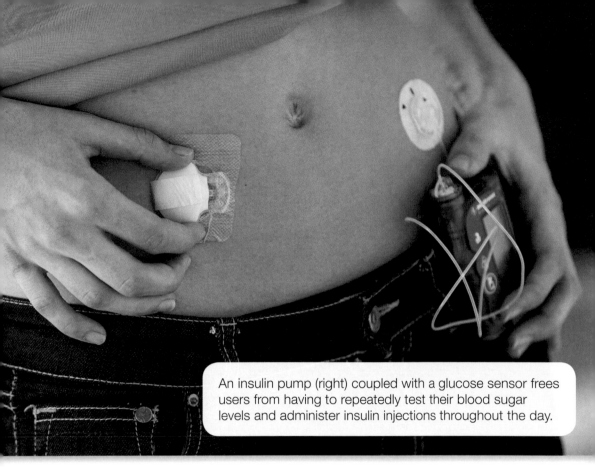

An insulin pump (right) coupled with a glucose sensor frees users from having to repeatedly test their blood sugar levels and administer insulin injections throughout the day.

a finger to get a drop of blood that can be placed on a strip and inserted into a meter that measures blood sugar. The meter reading lets the person know if glucose is too high or too low. Then the insulin injection is adjusted to that reading. Often people have to go through this procedure eight or ten times a day. Marquez hated the whole process and always had sore fingers, too. She says of her new pump, "This is so much better. This suits my lifestyle perfectly. I love school. I love to watch TV and hang out with my friends. I can do so many things without having to worry about my blood sugar. It would be really hard for me to go to a concert and draw some insulin with a syringe during the show. With this, it's just a click of the button. My life is so much easier."[21]

No matter how the insulin is delivered, the goal of insulin therapy is to keep glucose levels as close to normal as possible, twenty-four hours a day. On average, this means a blood glucose level from 80 mg/dL to 130 mg/dL before meals and a number no greater than

An Artificial Pancreas

At the end of 2016, an artificial pancreas device was approved by the US government for use by people with type 1 diabetes. The small device is worn on the abdomen. It has a pump for insulin delivery plus a sensor that communicates continuously with the pump about blood glucose levels. The sensor tells the pump to deliver insulin as needed without the need for the wearer to do or measure anything. The whole thing runs with a smartphone app that monitors how well it is working. Medical experts around the world have hailed the artificial pancreas as a breakthrough that will dramatically improve the lives of people who have type 1 diabetes.

In 2017 thirty-two teens experimented with using the artificial pancreas at a ski camp during intense exercise. Such exercise frequently causes hypoglycemia when people are unable to accurately judge how much insulin to inject. However, the teens using the artificial pancreas were able to maintain stable glucose levels. Zach Jonas, a Kansas City teen, got his new artificial pancreas in 2017 and loves the freedom it gives him. He explains, "If I go high, it gives me extra insulin, and if I go low, it cuts off the insulin flow, so my blood sugar naturally raises." Some biotechnology companies are planning to introduce devices by the end of 2018 that can also administer glucagon automatically and raise glucose levels when needed. Then the artificial pancreas would be able to do almost everything a normal pancreas can do.

Quoted in Abby Eden, "KC Teen with Diabetes Says New One-of-a-Kind Technology Has Given Him the Gift of Independence," Fox4KC.com, November 28, 2017. http://fox4kc.com.

180 mg/dL two hours after a meal. To accomplish this goal, people with type 1 use a variety of insulins. Rapid-acting insulin is taken before a meal to deal with the glucose rise that comes with food. It begins to take effect within ten minutes of injection and lasts three to five hours. Long-acting insulin starts working in about an hour and can last up to twenty-four hours. It is taken once or twice a day to help keep glucose levels stable. Short- and intermediate-acting insulin may also be used during the daytime if needed when rapid-acting insulin has worn off or long-acting insulin is not effective enough. Which kinds of insulin people use depends on their individual circumstances and how their bodies respond to insulin

therapy. Medical scientists have found that combinations of rapid- and long-acting insulins mimic the body's normal insulin use. Multiple daily injections with different acting insulins work better than just a couple of shots a day.

Managing Highs and Lows

Insulin therapy works well to manage glucose levels in the blood, but nothing works as well as a healthy pancreas. The normal pancreas matches the amount of insulin released to the amount of glucose in the blood. No injection can do that, so people with type 1 must test their glucose levels often or frequently check their CGMs. Especially at mealtimes, they count the carbs they are about to eat and then inject the right amount of insulin to cope with those carbs. For people with type 1, keeping track of glucose levels is critical, not only to prevent hyperglycemia but also to avoid the dangers of hypoglycemia.

Hypoglycemia is low blood glucose. It occurs when the balance of glucose to insulin in the blood is disrupted. Type 1 diabetes is complicated to control and can be unpredictable. Exercise, for example, can use up more glucose than expected, eating too few carbs at a meal can upset the balance, and injecting too much insulin can drop glucose levels way too far. Untreated hypoglycemia causes serious symptoms such as sweating, shakiness, dizziness, headache, and blurred vision. If allowed to continue, it can lead to confusion, behavior changes, convulsions, unconsciousness, and a condition called insulin shock, which can be life-threatening. People with type 1 learn to recognize the symptoms of hypoglycemia and, if they have a CGM, to set the device to beep a warning alert when glucose falls below a certain level. The immediate treatment for hypoglycemia is to ingest something sugary that will cause a rapid rise in glucose, such as a sweet snack, sugary juice, or a glucose tablet. Everyone with type 1 has to cope with episodes of low blood sugar.

Hyperglycemia is a common problem, too, and people with type 1 have to be aware of the symptoms, such as fatigue, increased thirst, blurred vision, increased urination, and hunger. After a glucose level test, the treatment is an additional dose of insulin. Hyperglycemia is often caused by eating the wrong kinds of food or by eating too much food. This means type 1 treatment involves lifelong careful meal planning and diet, as well as insulin therapy. For the most part, young people with diabetes can eat the same healthy diet that everyone should eat, but they do have to be more careful about high-sugar foods and excessive carbohydrates because these raise blood glucose levels easily and quickly. This does not mean that they can never have a baked potato or a piece of cake, but it does mean that they have to

Episodes of low blood sugar are common for those with type 1 diabetes. Consuming a sweet snack or sugary juice will quickly raise glucose levels and prevent hypoglycemia.

learn to count the carbs in each serving and then adjust the insulin bolus to the number of carbs they plan to eat. It does mean eating healthy fruits, vegetables, and proteins most of the time, choosing carbs that are digested more slowly, such as whole grains and beans, and eating meals that balance carbs with other foods, such as proteins and fats. It also means not skipping meals and eating unhealthy snacks only in moderation. When children with type 1 are young, their parents usually keep track of their diets and count their carbs. Older children and teens can do this themselves.

Type 2 Diabetes and Lifestyle Management

Treatment for type 2 diabetes also includes lifestyle changes in diet and exercise. The goal of type 2 treatment is to decrease insulin resistance, improve insulin production, and prevent the loss of beta cells over time. Since most young people diagnosed with type 2 are overweight, healthier eating habits are an important part of treatment. As with type 1, people with type 2 are encouraged to choose nutritious foods such as vegetables, fruits, whole grains, and proteins. They must try to avoid high-calorie sugary and fatty snacks and fast foods while limiting portion sizes of even healthy foods to the calorie amounts that they need for growth and health. Such a diet does not mean never having desserts or pizza, but it does mean consuming those empty calories only occasionally. Most medical professionals recommend eliminating high-sugar sodas completely because they raise glucose levels so quickly. The advantage of a healthy diet is weight loss, and weight loss is a critical way to reduce insulin resistance. Avoiding high-carb and sugary foods also helps keep glucose levels under control, which means reducing the risk of the complications of hyperglycemia.

Daily physical activity and exercise are of great benefit in helping a person control blood glucose levels, too. Activity increases metabolism and makes muscle cells more sensitive to insulin. As the glucose in the blood is used for fuel during exercise, blood sugar levels drop, and as calories are burned during activity, excess fat is reduced. Doctors believe that it is unhealthy for young people to lose weight by going on severely calorie-restricted diets. Instead, they recommend using exercise to burn more calories and eating a normal amount of healthy foods.

Type 2 and Medications

Some young people with type 2 are treated with lifestyle therapy alone, but for most, this is not enough. According to one study, only about 23 percent are able to maintain good control of glucose levels for two years without additional medical treatment. For adults, many different kinds of diabetes medications are available that work in several different ways to control blood glucose levels. For children and teens, however, only two diabetes medications are approved for use because so few studies have been done on the efficacy and safety of drugs in people under age eighteen. These two drugs are insulin and metformin. Metformin is an oral drug, taken in pill form. It helps reduce blood

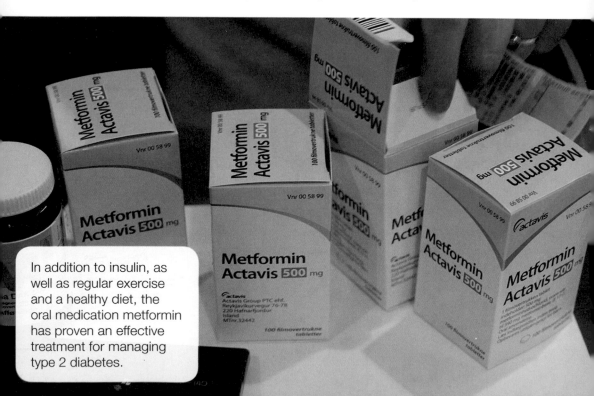

In addition to insulin, as well as regular exercise and a healthy diet, the oral medication metformin has proven an effective treatment for managing type 2 diabetes.

Treatment for Type 2 Complications

Many young people with type 2 diabetes are at risk for complications such as high blood pressure, high cholesterol and triglyceride levels (fats in the blood), and early kidney damage. If a child or teen has any signs of these disorders, the disorders are treated along with the diabetes. For kidney problems or high blood pressure, most diabetes doctors recommend a daily dose of a medication known as an ACE inhibitor. ACE inhibitors increase blood flow by helping blood vessels relax and dilate, thus lowering the work that the heart has to do and reducing blood pressure. This action also helps kidneys work better, more easily filtering blood that flows through them and reducing the risk of kidney damage. Drugs called statins are used to lower the excessive concentrations of fats in the blood. These fats, such as cholesterol and triglycerides, can eventually stick to blood vessel walls and clog them. If blood vessels develop blockages from the fatty deposits, the situation can cause heart disease and heart attacks. Successful treatment of diabetes must address not only glucose control but also any accompanying problems that can develop especially quickly in teens.

glucose levels in two ways: It decreases insulin resistance and also reduces the amount of glucose released by the liver, where extra glucose is stored. Along with diet and exercise, metformin can bring blood glucose under control and into normal ranges. Generally, people start metformin at a relatively low dose taken twice a day, but the doses can be increased if average glucose levels remain too high.

Many young people with type 2 need to inject insulin along with taking metformin because their beta cells simply cannot provide enough insulin to avoid hyperglycemia. Doctors usually recommend insulin if blood glucose levels are at 250 mg/dL or higher. Those who inject insulin must test their blood glucose levels and be aware of the dangers of hypoglycemia, just like people with type 1. Most test their glucose levels at least three times a day. The major difference is that young people with type 2 may be able to reduce or even eliminate insulin therapy if they watch their diets and lose weight. John Perrone, for example, was an overweight eleven-year-old when he was diagnosed with type 2 diabetes. He needed insulin therapy to keep his blood sugar under control. Perrone worked hard to lose weight and become physically fit. By the time he was fifteen, he had reached the point that he no longer needed insulin injections. He controls his diabetes with diet, activity, and metformin. Perrone explains, "It's all about in and out, what you eat, how much you exercise."[22]

> "It's all about in and out, what you eat, how much you exercise."[22]
>
> —John Perrone, who has type 2 diabetes

Other people may not be able to eliminate insulin therapy but can still become healthier. Sixteen-year-old Annie Snyder, for example, lost 12 pounds (5.4 kg) in the first year of her diagnosis by reducing the carbohydrates in her diet and exercising. Because of that weight loss, she was able to cut her insulin injections from several a day to just one nightly injection of long-acting insulin. Snyder explains, "Before, exercise was a chore. I would sit and watch TV and eat snacks. Now, as soon as I come home, I put on my workout clothes."[23]

The Burden of Diabetes Treatment

Treating type 2 in young people is complex, and each individual responds to treatment differently. Many children and teens cannot cope with the lifestyle changes and medications that are necessary to manage diabetes. Some research suggests that the failure rate for treatment plans for youth is as high as 60 percent. People are unable to lose weight, forget to test their glucose levels, or cannot tolerate always having to watch what they eat. Their diabetes and hyperglycemia get worse. People with type 1 diabetes face some of these problems, too. The trouble is that diabetes treatment is burdensome and demanding and requires constant vigilance. Even when treatment is successful, it is never easy, and it never takes the diabetes away.

Chapter 4

What Is It Like to Live with Diabetes?

va Hata is eleven years old and has had type 1 diabetes since she was eighteen months old. She says that living with diabetes all her life has taught her how to be strong and independent, despite the difficulties she faces. Hata knows how to take care of herself. She recalls, "I remember the first time I pricked myself. I was about 4 years old, and I hated being dependent on other people to prick my finger. I snuck into my bedroom and did it based on what I had observed my parents doing. After that day, the momentum of learning to do it all by myself really took off. . . . I have learned what to do and when to do it."[24]

Hata lives a full and busy life despite diabetes. She loves literature and learning about history. She rides horses and is interested in showing and training dogs. She enjoys building things, like terrariums and playhouses. And she owns a diabetes alert dog named Bruin that she trained herself. The dog accompanies her everywhere and is able to sense and alert her when she has a high or low. The dog does this by detecting the odor of chemicals released by her body when hypoglycemic or hyperglycemic episodes are occurring. Because of Bruin, who

Twin sisters who have diabetes attend an award ceremony recognizing their service dog. Diabetic alert dogs are trained to sense and alert when their owners' blood sugar is too high or too low.

acts something like a CGM, Hata is free to pursue her outdoor lifestyle without worrying about getting into difficulty when she is by herself. Nevertheless, Hata is well aware that she has to adjust to life with a chronic disease. She says, "First of all, people need to understand that it's not simple and although you think there is a 'control' with diabetes, there isn't—and won't be until there's a cure."[25]

The Shock of a Diabetes Diagnosis

Learning to live with a chronic disease that can be managed but not completely controlled can be hard. Hata has done so for as long as she can remember, but for many people a diabetes diagnosis comes as a shock. It can take time and effort to get used to living with a new reality, even though most people eventually learn to live with diabetes with grace and determination. Elka Karl, for example, clearly remembers how angry and sad she was when she was diagnosed with type 1 at age sixteen. She had lost 20 pounds (9.1 kg) over the previous two months in addition to feeling fatigued, extra thirsty, and just generally weak and sick. When she had her blood glucose tested, it was over 300 mg/dL, and she was immediately hospitalized. Karl was overwhelmed by the diagnosis at first. She says:

> "Although you think there is a 'control' with diabetes, there isn't—and won't be until there's a cure."[25]
>
> —Ava Hata, who has type 1 diabetes

That first day in the hospital, I curled up into a little ball and cried. . . . Doctors came and I glared at them until my chin trembled with poorly disguised despair. Visitors arrived and I hurriedly sent them away. My entire high school marching band marched from school to the hospital, instruments in hand, to wish me well, and I could only give them the most cursory of thank yous before collapsing into tears.[26]

Quite quickly, Karl became determined to take care of herself. She learned to give herself insulin injections and to test her glucose levels, but she was scared. Once she was back at school, she quit her karate classes because the activity caused frightening hypoglycemia episodes, and she did not know how to cope. She explains, "I gave up too quickly—I know that now—but at the time, it was all too much. I was desperate for safety, and any activity that so quickly turned me into a shaking, sweating, discombobulated mess terrified me."[27] Karl thought that her normal life was over, and it took her some months to overcome those initial fears and learn to manage the scary lows. A year later, for instance, she was on a long hike when her blood glucose level dropped to 21 mg/dL. She gamely struggled back to her car, where she always kept sugary snacks, ate the food she needed, got her glucose back up, and calmly drove home.

Too Much Fear

Brittnay DeClouette was panic stricken when she was diagnosed with diabetes, too, but since she was only ten, her fears were somewhat different than Karl's. She remembers thinking, "Isn't that the disease from those scary commercials? Didn't the old babysitter have that? And didn't she have to take . . . SHOTS?" DeClouette became used to the insulin shots and the finger pricks for testing. She learned that she could handle the discomfort and the complications of the disease. She says now, "Battling diabetes has given me motivation to pursue my goals. It's humbled me. It has made me who I am today."[28]

Some people, though, take longer to get over the fear. Seventeen-year-old Sierra Pettigrew lives in Kentucky. Her father has diabetes, and he was the one who noticed one evening that she had to go to the bathroom five times in a single hour. Concerned, he checked her blood glucose with his meter and discovered that it was high. When she went to the hospital the next day, her meter reading was 689 mg/dL. She was diagnosed with type 2 diabetes and immediately started on insulin therapy. Over the next six months, Pettigrew learned how to competently take care of herself. She learned to test her blood glucose, to give herself injections before meals and at bedtime, and to change her diet. She started swimming and walking for exercise and continued to play her favorite sport of basketball at school. She lost weight and cooperated fully with her treatment plan.

Nevertheless, Pettigrew cannot shake the fear that she is unsafe. She knows the teachers at school watch out for her, but

> "Battling diabetes has given me motivation to pursue my goals. . . . It has made me who I am today."[28]
>
> —Brittnay DeClouette, who has type 1 diabetes

Dating and Diabetes

For many teens, deciding whether or when to tell a dating partner about having diabetes is difficult. The American Diabetes Association (ADA) advises that there is no right or wrong answer to this question. Each teen can make his or her own choice. Some teens prefer privacy, and that is OK. Others do not mind telling a trusted dating partner about the disease. The ADA offers some tips for those who make the choice to share. One suggestion is to keep the information simple. For instance, a teen might say to a date, "I have diabetes so I have to plan a little when I eat. I keep track of my blood glucose levels and give myself insulin." The ADA also explains that most people are "very caring and concerned" and are unlikely to judge anyone negatively about having diabetes. However, the ADA does warn that people are curious, too. It suggests that when a teen makes the decision to share about having diabetes, he or she should "be ready to answer a lot of questions. In fact, that's a good sign—and it could mean a second date!"

American Diabetes Association, "Dating," October 21, 2013. www.diabetes.org.

after school she does not like to go out much on her own anymore. She has experienced hypoglycemic episodes that were frightening, and she wants to be where her mother can help her if it happens. She wants to stay home with the safety of having her parents close by. Pettigrew says, "I'm kind of worried about being far away from my mom. I told her I'm never moving out."[29] Pettigrew's mother tries to encourage her to be more independent, but adjusting to the limitations of diabetes treatment is not easy.

Treatment Struggles

Even young people who have adjusted well to managing their diabetes can have emotional issues with the complexity of treatment plans. Yazzy, for instance, says, "I hate having diabetes. . . . I hate being different and having to come out of my way to do injections and prick my fingers, it's horrible."[30] Annie was diagnosed with diabetes when she was six years old. She is seventeen now, but she says she struggles emotionally with having the disease. For years, she even hated the word *diabetes* and always called it "the d word" instead. She suffered with depression about her situation, crying a lot and fearing being defined by her diabetes instead of being appreciated for who she is. She is better now, but she admits, "I still hate it and it makes me angry and upset. I just wish I didn't have it."[31]

Seventeen-year-old Chloe, on the other hand, has good days and bad days. She explains, "I know some days it gets a bit hard and a bit tedious, and it's sort of like you sit there and think, why on earth did it [diabetes] pick me? Did it ever think that maybe I don't want to do injections every day? Did it ever think that maybe I just wanted to live life the way all my friends live life? But most days, living with diabetes is okay, you soon get used to it."[32]

Burnout

When children are young, parents are largely responsible for the vigilance and discipline necessary for managing and controlling diabetes. Once children are around ten years old, they usually start taking on the responsibility themselves, and many can be independent by the time they are in their teens. Some teens, however, may rebel against the never-ending demands and simply become tired of dealing with diabetes. The Joslin Diabetes Center says, "In many cases, these teens have had to deal with insulin injections, carb counting, and the fear of overnight lows for years. It's very likely that at some point, they'll just want to quit. . . . Throw into the mix shifting blood glucose numbers and social issues related to being different from peers, and frustration with the situation can lead to something called diabetes burnout."[33]

People with diabetes burnout may skip insulin injections, stop checking their blood glucose levels, and eat meals high in carbs—and hide these activities from their parents and medical caregivers. Hadley George experienced this burnout as a freshman in high school, after living with type 1 since she was four years old. She remembers:

By the time high school arrived, I was fed up with diabetes. Like any other teenager, I wanted to fit in and be a part of the cool crowd. As you can imagine, I was unlike any of my friends; none of them had an insulin pump attached to their hip or had to prick their finger every time they ate. I wanted a boyfriend, but what boy would ever date me, with all this baggage? I wanted to wear a pretty dress, but could never find a place to hide my insulin pump. I wanted a good night's rest, but was woken up to test my blood every night. In my eyes, diabetes stopped me from being a normal person. I was passed the pissed off stage and arrived at the stage of sadness and disappointment. I decided the most logical solution to my problems was to ignore diabetes entirely. I stopped checking my blood sugar and would randomly bolus [inject an insulin dose] when I could feel my blood sugar rise.[34]

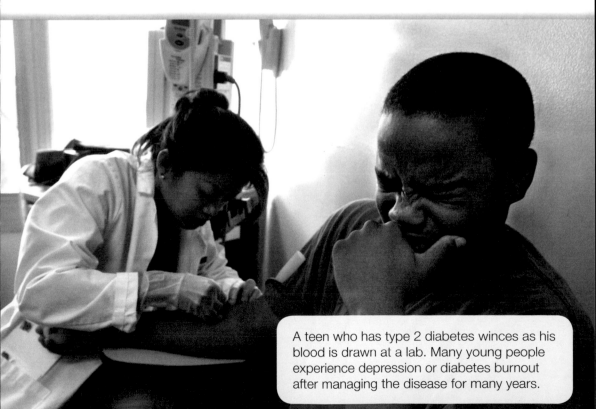

A teen who has type 2 diabetes winces as his blood is drawn at a lab. Many young people experience depression or diabetes burnout after managing the disease for many years.

George thinks that it is inevitable for every teen with diabetes to go through burnout at some point, simply because everyone "gets tired of the endless attention diabetes requires." As her continually rising hyperglycemia made her feel sicker and sicker, George was able to get past her burnout. She decided that she could either die from her diabetes or take control of it and "not let diabetes win."[35] And today, she uses her experiences with overcoming burnout to help other teens going through the same problems.

Lauren Stanford experienced burnout, too, but for her it consisted of seven years of off-again, on-again efforts to ignore her diabetes. She remembers being twelve years old and lying to her mother about checking her blood glucose during a swim meet. She pretended she had checked her glucose and told her mother

Through Burnout and Back

Camilla Rossil has lived with type 1 diabetes since she was four years old. She is in her thirties now and living a positive, healthy life, but she spent years as a teen and young adult plagued with burnout. She wanted to be like her friends, and as a teen, she stopped injecting insulin and checking her glucose levels. Soon she had to be hospitalized. She remembers, "I was 15 at the time and attended a party where I drank way too much alcohol. As I had 'forgotten' to take insulin, I got really very sick and vomited for three days. The doctors later told me that, had I arrived at the hospital two hours later, I would have gone into a coma and never woken up again. I was really shocked." The girl was scared into taking care of her diabetes until college, when she again let her treatment slide as she traveled, studied, and enjoyed student life. Finally, the complications of her uncontrolled diabetes led to blindness. It took six eye surgeries to partially restore her sight.

Today, Rossil is healthy and independent, and she takes excellent care of herself. She no longer rebels against having diabetes. She says, "I love my life. Despite all the challenges I've had to overcome, I think my life is amazing. I intend to live a long and happy life. I think I'll live until I'm 105 years old."

Quoted in Birgit Ottermann, "Life with Diabetes: I Want to Live Until I'm 105," Health24 Diabetes, February 20, 2017. www.health24.com.

that the number was good. In reality, she did not use her meter at all. She recalls:

> I was just plain sick of checking my blood sugar. I thought, *what's the harm in skipping?* The reward is I can pretend diabetes isn't there. . . . I started off as just lying about my blood sugars, then it turned into lying about giving myself insulin, there was even a phase when I would take my pump off for periods of time without taking any injections. I realized even then that my behavior was destructive, but I cannot tell you how nice it was to just eat a meal without the brouhaha of doing so with diabetes. The freedom of being able to just not deal with diabetes is incredibly liberating and, unfortunately, severely addictive. One might argue that feeling terrible all the time isn't worth the freedom of not having to do all those tedious tasks, and I can agree with you now, but back then, it was worth it for me.[36]

Stanford and George were fortunate that their burnout periods did not cause serious problems. Twelve-year-old Moha was not as lucky. She has had type 1 for ten years and did well as a young child. But, she explains,

> as I grew older . . . I kept noticing that none of my friends had to test their bloods or do their injections like I did. So I started to skip injections and drink fizzy drinks and eat more and more sugar and fats and lying to the doctors who wanted to help me. I was losing weight and was hospitalized at least 3 times because of my recklessness. But one visit to the clinic changed my life. My doctor said I was starting to leak protein in my urine, which meant my kidneys were starting to fail. Luckily, the hospital said because I was young, I could reverse this just by cutting down on the bad food and testing my blood and doing my injections. . . . Thank God I stopped harming myself before I did any real damage.[37]

Needing Support

Some young people are not really burned out, but they do struggle with being different from their friends and family and having to give up so many foods that other people can enjoy. This, too, can mean having trouble managing diabetes. Seventeen-year-old Carolina Torres, for example, has coped with type 2 diabetes since she was eleven. Her mother has diabetes, too. Both Torres and her mother have trouble sticking to the right diet because it means giving up the foods they love and resisting frequent temptations. Torres explains, "It's a struggle sometimes because my brother doesn't have diabetes so he loves eating fried chicken or stuff that is very greasy or very high in sugars. Me and my mom, we try our best but the temptation is always there and so sometimes it's harder."[38]

When the family is supportive, it makes all the difference for anybody who is managing diabetes. Annie Snyder, for instance, had the strong support of her family when she was diagnosed with type 2. Her parents turned the dining room into an exercise room and got rid of all the junk food in the house. Even Snyder's brother drinks bottled water instead of soda and exercises. The whole family works out every day. Snyder says, "When I see my dad exercise, I know that I've helped get him motivated."[39] And knowing she has helped her family get healthy motivates Snyder as well. Minnie Ortiz also credits her family's support for her successful management of diabetes. She explains, "My family is the real reason I have survived this. They motivate me, and if it wasn't for them, I wouldn't feel pushed to control my diabetes. They've even started eating healthier too."[40]

> "My family is the real reason I have survived this."[40]
>
> —Minnie Ortiz, who has type 2 diabetes

Embracing the Difference

How one's peers react to diabetes affects everyone trying to live with the disease. Sometimes people are bullied or teased at school

Having a supportive family who engages in healthy activities together can make managing diabetes easier.

because they are different, have to go to the nurse's office for an injection, or wear an insulin pump. These reactions can make life miserable and make it hard to accept having diabetes. Other times, friends and their support are a tremendous help. Sarah Ball, for example, was thirteen years old when she developed type 1 and felt embarrassed and ashamed about her differences at school. She tried to hide her condition from everyone. When a friend saw her testing her blood sugar and asked what the meter was, Ball froze in shame and ignored the question. Ball says, "Later that day, she messaged me and I explained that I was a diabetic and I didn't want her to think I was a freak because I wasn't like everyone else. She responded with compassion and explained how she would have never thought that, even if I am different. I started to feel better about being different after that conversation."[41]

Ball is eighteen now, and as most people with diabetes eventually do, she has learned to accept diabetes and not be embarrassed about who she is. She explains:

> As I grew up and realized that differences are what make us interesting, I started to embrace diabetes. . . . After 5 years with diabetes, I still notice the stares in public when I check my blood sugar. And notice people staring at my waist, but my outlook has changed. I wear my insulin pump proudly and answer questions with confidence. I help people understand that it isn't uncommon or weird. . . . And it's okay to be a bit different.[42]

Chapter 5

Can Diabetes Be Prevented?

enes may play a large role in the development of diabetes, but heredity is not necessarily destiny. Medical researchers are working to determine the environmental factors that trigger diabetes in vulnerable people. They know they may not be able to prevent every case of diabetes, and they cannot change genes, but these scientists believe that a great reduction in the incidence of the disease is possible and will become a reality in the future.

Type 1 Prevention Research

With type 1 diabetes, researchers are trying to prevent or at least delay the onset of the disease for many years in genetically vulnerable children. One prevention method being studied involves trying to prevent the loss of beta cells. Medical scientists have discovered that type 1 does not come on suddenly, even though it is typically diagnosed after just a few weeks of symptoms and sickness. Long before that time, changes are happening in the body that lead to diabetes. The first step in the onset of diabetes is the immune system developing at least two autoantibodies.

These are antibodies against the self—in this case, against the beta cells of the pancreas. The immune system has been activated and begun to mount the attack against beta cells. At this stage few beta cells have been affected, and the person has no symptoms of disease. Doctors can identify autoantibodies circulating in the bloodstream with a simple blood test.

The next step in diabetes progression is that enough beta cells have died to cause biological changes. Blood glucose levels rise, but the person still has enough beta cells to prevent any symptoms of illness. Unless that person happens to get a blood sugar test, no one knows that anything is amiss. It is not until the last step in diabetes progression—when most beta cells have been killed—that a person develops obvious symptoms of diabetes. By that time it is too late to prevent diabetes, but researchers believe that catching the autoimmune problem early might mean saving enough beta cells to keep diabetes from occurring, or at least delay it for several years.

Today both the ADA and the JDRF (formerly the Juvenile Diabetes Research Foundation) recommend that anyone with relatives with type 1 be screened for autoantibodies. Even if they do not test positive for autoantibodies, children should be tested every year until age eighteen. Such screening would not catch everyone who will develop type 1, but since diabetes is known to run in families, the screening is a good tool for preventing some cases of the disease. The screening is offered by a research group known as TrialNet, which is funded by the National Institute of Diabetes and Digestive and Kidney Diseases (NIDDK). TrialNet's chair, Dr. Carla Greenbaum, explains, "We have several therapies that can interfere with the disease process, and we need to continue to study this so that we can find new therapies for people with diabetes."[43]

> "We need to continue to study this so that we can find new therapies for people with diabetes."[43]
>
> —Dr. Carla Greenbaum

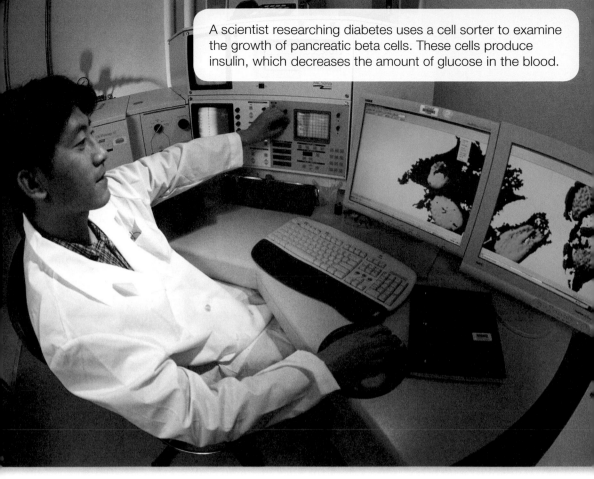

A scientist researching diabetes uses a cell sorter to examine the growth of pancreatic beta cells. These cells produce insulin, which decreases the amount of glucose in the blood.

All the therapies available so far are a part of clinical trials. People volunteer to enroll in one of these studies to see if different interventions will prevent the disease. One of the ongoing clinical trials is studying the effects of a drug known as abatacept. Abatacept is already approved for use in children with autoimmune arthritis to help slow the autoimmune process. TrialNet researchers tried the drug with children already diagnosed with diabetes and discovered that it helped save the few beta cells these patients had left. That did not cure their diabetes, but the researchers think that it might preserve the beta cells in children who do not yet have diabetes symptoms. The researchers are administering abatacept to people age six and older who have two or more autoantibodies in their blood but still have normal glucose levels. The study will continue for years, but the researchers are hopeful that in the end they will have found a way to prevent beta cell loss and preserve insulin in children who otherwise have a 100 percent risk of developing diabetes.

Finland's Vaccine

In Finland researchers are taking a different approach to preventing type 1 diabetes: They are experimenting with a vaccine. Finland has one of the highest incidences of type 1 diabetes in the world. Although there are many theories as to why so many Finns have type 1, no one knows the true cause. Finland's medical sci-

Must Society Change?

Some public health experts argue that type 2 diabetes can be prevented only with changes in social attitudes and government actions that target nutrition and diet. They argue, for example, that many children and teens live in dense urban areas where physical activity and exercise are too difficult because there are no safe, comfortable places to play or participate in sports. Communities need to be planned with parks and other recreational areas so that everyone can lead an active lifestyle.

These experts also suggest that government campaigns, such as those that successfully discouraged tobacco usage, are needed to discourage excessive television, video game, and phone time. Perhaps, they argue, public awareness of the dangers of sedentary activities could be raised with government advertising campaigns and public service announcements. Public health experts also suggest government actions that discourage unhealthy food choices. For instance, they suggest higher taxes on unhealthy foods like fast foods and sodas to encourage people to make healthier choices. Experts Jaakko Tuomilehto and Peter E.H. Schwarz even suggest "a policy of liability of food and beverage companies for adverse health events associated with the use of their products." That would mean people who developed diseases like type 2 diabetes could sue soda companies for contributing to their illness. No one expects such changes in regulations and public policies to happen quickly, but many thoughtful people speculate that they might be necessary.

Jaakko Tuomilehto and Peter E.H. Schwarz, "Preventing Diabetes: Early Versus Late Preventive Interventions," *Diabetes Care*, August 2016, p. S118. http://care.diabetesjournals.org.

entists, however, place a high priority on diabetes research and figuring out how to reverse their epidemic of diabetes cases. After twenty-five years of experimental research and study, researchers at the University of Tampere have linked a specific virus called the coxsackievirus B1 to an autoimmune reaction and type 1 diabetes in some people.

Coxsackievirus B1 is a kind of enterovirus. Enteroviruses cause many kinds of diseases and grow in the intestinal tract. They are very common, are highly infectious, and cause millions of illnesses around the world each year. Coxsackievirus B1 infections are particularly common in children, even newborns. Some scientists say that perhaps the antigens on the virus are similar to those on beta cells, causing a mistaken immune system attack. Others suggest that enteroviruses may be attracted to the pancreas and chronically infect its cells, thus causing the immune system to attack. However the virus works, it seems that it may trigger vulnerable immune systems to begin attacking beta cells.

In 2014 University of Tampere researchers successfully developed a vaccine against coxsackievirus B1. The first step was to test the vaccine in mice, and it did indeed protect the mice from being infected by the virus. A vaccine cannot cure people (or mice) who are already infected, but it can prevent the infection in the first place. It works by causing the immune system to develop antibodies against a specific infection. Should a person ever be exposed to that infection, the antibodies quickly trigger an immune system attack that prevents any infection from taking place. The germs are destroyed before they can do any harm.

If genetically vulnerable children never were infected by coxsackievirus B1, researchers believe, it is likely that they would never develop type 1 diabetes. Even if coxsackievirus B1 is not the only infectious virus that triggers diabetes, preventing it could prevent many cases of type 1. Professor Mikael Knip, one of the lead researchers, says, "This vaccine could prevent at least half of new cases."[44] Trials of the new vaccine in humans began in Finland in 2018. The trial will have to continue for at least eight years so that researchers can follow the vaccinated children to see if they develop diabetes. Nevertheless, the researchers hope that their vaccine will be a breakthrough in the prevention of type 1 diabetes in the future.

Type 2 and Prevention

Preventing type 2 diabetes is unlikely to involve vaccines, but the medical world agrees that at least 50 percent of type 2 cases could be prevented with lifestyle changes. These lifestyle changes are much the same as those recommended for people diagnosed with diabetes, but experts believe that healthy lifestyles could prevent diabetes in most young people altogether, or at least delay its onset for many years into adulthood. Type 2 diabetes used to be rare in children because being overweight and inactive was rare. Now the CDC predicts that unless Western culture's lifestyle is changed, one out of every three children born after the year 2000 will develop diabetes during their lifetime.

Writing for the ADA's journal *Diabetes Care*, Jaakko Tuomilehto and Peter E.H. Schwarz argue, "Today, we live in a toxic food environment, which provides us with energy-dense and cheap food 24 h[ours] a day and exposes us to aggressive marketing campaigns that promote the consumption of unhealthy food items."[45] Energy-dense foods are those that are high in fat and sugar. They are very filling and have a lot of calories but are not necessarily healthy. They are most often fast foods, snack foods, premade foods (such as boxed macaroni and cheese or frozen waffles), or sweets like candy, doughnuts, and cookies. They are foods that promote weight gain when they are eaten regularly. Tuomilehto and Schwarz believe that society should reject these foods and make it harder for people to buy them.

> "Today, we live in a toxic food environment, which provides us with energy-dense and cheap food."[45]
>
> —Jaakko Tuomilehto and Peter E.H. Schwarz, diabetes experts

Societies are unlikely to turn against unhealthy foods as a whole anytime soon, but the CDC offers recommendations to families who want to avoid the environmental risk factors for type 2 diabetes. For children and teens, it says that weight and activity matter. Healthy eating habits recommended by the CDC include drinking more water and fewer sodas and other sugary drinks, eating more fruits and vegetables (especially for snacks), cooking meals together as a family, and eating at the table instead of while watching television. One study found that young people lose weight when their time watching television is limited. This did not happen because they got more active. Instead, the CDC explains, "the difference was snacking: kids ate more when they were watching TV than when doing other activities, even sedentary (not physically active) ones."[46]

Encouraging children and teens to choose nutritious foods over junk food and soda can help to avoid or significantly delay the onset of type 2 diabetes.

The CDC also strongly encourages physical activity to reduce type 2 risk because activity improves the body's use of insulin and decreases insulin resistance. It recommends that every young person get at least sixty minutes of physical activity every day. Young people can take a fitness class, join a sports team, walk, hike, bike, or help with household chores such as raking leaves, vacuuming, or gardening. It recommends that screen time (television, video games, and phone use) be limited to two hours a day. Combining increased activity with healthier food choices can help people lose weight without resorting to strict dieting. And the loss of just a few pounds can reduce or at least delay the risk of developing type 2 diabetes. Even delaying the onset of diabetes for a few years is valuable because the longer a person has diabetes, the more likely he or she is to develop complications. The NIDDK explains, "You may be able to prevent or delay diabetes by losing 5 to 7 percent of your starting weight. For instance, if you weigh 200 pounds, your goal would be to lose about 10 to 14 pounds."[47]

> "You may be able to prevent or delay diabetes by losing 5 to 7 percent of your starting weight."[47]
>
> —The NIDDK

Starting Early

Everyone should strive for a healthy lifestyle, but for people with known risk factors for developing diabetes, good habits can be especially important. Young people who have family members with diabetes or who are members of certain ethnic groups may need medical intervention to prevent or delay diabetes. Medical researchers know that children who are Native American, Hispanic, Asian American, Pacific Islander, and African American are at particular risk, although no one knows why. Starting at age ten, children who are overweight and have other risk factors should have their blood glucose tested during their medical exams. They

To Reverse Insulin Resistance

If insulin resistance could be reversed, scientists say, people would not develop type 2 diabetes. Much research today is devoted to understanding what causes insulin resistance and learning how to fight it. In 2017 a group of researchers at the University of San Diego School of Medicine reported discovering one cause of insulin resistance. The team found that obesity causes immune system cells known as macrophages to invade fatty tissues. The macrophages react to the fat cells as if they are damaged or injured. They cause inflammation as they attack the fat cells and release chemicals that block the action of insulin in the cells. Then these same chemicals travel in the bloodstream and enter other body tissues, such as liver and muscle cells.

Using obese and slim mice, the researchers experimented with the macrophages' chemicals. They found that collecting them from obese mice and injecting them into slim mice caused the slim mice to develop insulin resistance. When they injected obese mice with chemicals from the fat cells of slim mice, which were not inflamed, the obese mice became sensitive to insulin. This research is important because it demonstrates that it might be possible to develop a treatment to stop the inflammation that leads to insulin resistance in people in the future. If insulin resistance were treatable, then type 2 diabetes could be prevented.

should be tested every three years after that to be sure that insulin resistance is not beginning. Testing blood glucose can reveal prediabetes, a condition in which glucose levels are higher than normal but not high enough to be called diabetes. Prediabetes often can be reversed and blood glucose brought into the normal range with weight loss and exercise. Then diabetes is prevented.

Around the country, clinics have been established to help prevent type 2 diabetes in America's youth. At the Youth Diabetes Prevention Program at Riley Children's Health of Indiana University, for example, a specialized medical team works to prevent diabetes in young people. People are usually referred to the program by their doctors. The team consists of specialized medical doctors, nurses, psychologists, dietitians, personal trainers, health coaches, and other professionals who develop

Young people who practice an active, healthy lifestyle from an early age can improve their body's use of insulin and may reduce their risk of type 2 diabetes.

an individualized treatment plan for each child or teen. Education about diabetes and prevention is also a part of the program, and the whole family is encouraged to participate. Goals are set up with the young person's input, and success is tracked regularly. The ultimate mission of programs such as the Youth Diabetes Prevention Program is to motivate people to lead healthy lifestyles and to greatly reduce the onset of type 2 diabetes in children and teens.

Intervention programs and lifestyle changes may work to prevent many cases of diabetes, but no one believes that type 2 can be prevented altogether. Medical help cannot change the genetics that are associated with diabetes. Even some risk factors are not amenable to intervention. For instance, researchers know that children who weighed less than 5 pounds (2.3 kg) or more than

10 pounds (4.5 kg) at birth are at greater risk for developing type 2 than other children. Babies born to mothers who had diabetes or obesity during pregnancy are more likely to develop type 2 as they grow up than are other children. Girls are more likely to develop type 2 at puberty than are boys. And different ethnic groups, perhaps because the populations share common genes, are more vulnerable to diabetes than others.

No one knows exactly why these risk factors are related to type 2 diabetes. No one is sure yet how to reduce the risk that these factors contribute to the onset of diabetes. In addition, some youth who develop diabetes are slim and do not have type 2 in their families. The causes or triggers in these cases are unclear. Even for children who are overweight, lifestyle changes may not always lead to a healthy weight. Most medical researchers believe that obesity is, in large part, controlled by inborn genetic variables. Many suspect that the genes that lead to being overweight may be some of the same genes that lead to type 2 diabetes. Controlling the actions of these genes with diet modifications is not simple or easy. Therefore, any efforts to prevent type 2 cannot be 100 percent successful.

No Shame

Many people with type 2 diabetes, whether they are children, teens, or adults, experience a social stigma about their disease. Mary Kemp, a diabetes educator, asks, "Have you ever been shamed and blamed right to your face for having type 2 diabetes?"[48] She says that it is common for society to think diabetes is a disease people cause in themselves by eating poorly or gaining weight, when in reality nothing could be further from the truth. The fact that treatment and prevention involve lifestyle changes does not mean that diabetes is anyone's fault. Kemp goes on to explain, "One thing to be very clear about, being overweight does not cause type 2 diabetes. Insulin resistance causes weight gain and type 2 diabetes."[49] The causes of diabetes are so complex that no one should feel bad about having it.

Because so few people really understand diabetes, even people with type 1 can face being stigmatized or feeling misunderstood by others. In one survey, 83 percent of parents of children with type 1 felt blamed for causing their children's disease. About 75 percent of people with type 1 also felt ashamed and embarrassed about having diabetes. In general, the public does not understand diabetes or realize that there are different forms. Education is needed so that what can and cannot be prevented is more widely understood. Today, however, the medical world has more hope than ever before that the future will bring the ability to prevent many people from facing the burden of living with diabetes.

"One thing to be very clear about, being overweight does not cause type 2 diabetes."[49]

—Mary Kemp, diabetes educator

Source Notes

Introduction: A Miraculous Success

1. Quoted in Austin Bunn, "The Way We Live Now: 3-16-03: Body Check; The Bittersweet Science," *New York Times Magazine*, March 16, 2003. www.nytimes.com.
2. *Toronto Daily Star*, "America's Leading Medical Scientists Unite in Lauding Insulin Extract," June 20, 1923, reprinted in Insulin Library, University of Toronto. https://insulin.library .utoronto.ca.

Chapter 1: What Is Diabetes?

3. Diabetes.co.uk, "Diabetes and Metabolism," 2018. www.dia betes.co.uk.
4. Marcia Frank and Denis Daneman, "Insulin: An Overview," Children's Hospital, London Health Sciences Centre, February 12, 2010. www.aboutkidshealth.ca.
5. Quoted in Laura Dean and Johanna McEntyre, *The Genetic Landscape of Diabetes*. Bethesda, MD: National Center for Biotechnology Information, 2004, p. 14.
6. Quoted in Diabetes UK, "Your Stories in Brief," 2017. www .diabetes.org.uk.
7. Quoted in Diabetes UK, "Your Stories in Brief."
8. Brittnay DeClouette, "A Weekend Excursion to a Type 1 Diabetes Diagnosis," ASweetLife, March 19, 2015. https://as weetlife.org.

9. Minnie Ortiz, "One Patient's Story: My Type 2 Diabetes," Boston Children's Hospital, December 18, 2009. https://thriving .childrenshospital.org.

10. Jason Fung, "What, Exactly, Is Insulin Resistance?—T2D 23," Intensive Dietary Management, 2018. https://idmprogram.com.

Chapter 2: What Causes Diabetes?

11. Dean and McEntyre, *The Genetic Landscape of Diabetes*, p. 1.

12. Quoted in Diabetes UK, "Your Stories in Brief."

13. Quoted in Joslin Diabetes Center, "Genetics & Diabetes: What's Your Risk?," 2018. www.joslin.org.

14. Quoted in Editor, "Early Trauma 'Triples' Risk of Type 1 Diabetes," *Diabetes Times*, April 9, 2015. http://diabetestimes .co.uk.

15. Quoted in Editor, "Early Trauma 'Triples' Risk of Type 1 Diabetes."

16. Centers for Disease Control and Prevention, "Defining Childhood Obesity," October 20, 2016. www.cdc.gov.

17. David Mendosa, "Diabetes Genes," Mendosa.com, August 17, 2005. www.mendosa.com.

Chapter 3: Can Diabetes Be Treated or Cured?

18. Megan Coleman, "A Day in the Life of a Type 1 Diabetic," Odyssey, November 2, 2015. www.theodysseyonline.com.

19. Coleman, "A Day in the Life of a Type 1 Diabetic."

20. Coleman, "A Day in the Life of a Type 1 Diabetic."

21. Quoted in Victor R. Martinez, "Insulin Pump Makes Life Easier for Teen with Diabetes," *El Paso (TX) Times*, March 6, 2016. www.elpasotimes.com.

22. Quoted in Susan Brink, "Type 2 Diabetes Surges in People Younger than 20," *Washington Post*, March 21, 2011. www .washingtonpost.com.

23. Quoted in Brink, "Type 2 Diabetes Surges in People Younger than 20."

Chapter 4: What Is It Like to Live with Diabetes?

24. Quoted in *CHOC Children's* (blog), "Living with Diabetes: One Child's Perspective," Children's Hospital of Orange County, November 29, 2016. https://blog.chocchildrens.org.

25. Quoted in *CHOC Children's* (blog), "Living with Diabetes."

26. Elka Karl, "My Way-Too-Sweet Sixteen: A Type 1 Diabetes Diagnosis Story," ASweetLife, January 25, 2017. https://asweetlife.org.

27. Karl, "My Way-Too-Sweet Sixteen."

28. DeClouette, "A Weekend Excursion to a Type 1 Diabetes Diagnosis."

29. Quoted in Laura Ungar, "Teen Adjusts to Life with Type 2 Diabetes," *Louisville (KY) Courier Journal*, November 14, 2016. www.courier-journal.com.

30. Quoted in Diabetes UK, "Your Stories in Brief."

31. Quoted in Diabetes UK, "Your Stories in Brief."

32. Quoted in Diabetes UK, "Your Stories in Brief."

33. Joslin Communications, "How to Help a Teen with Diabetes Burnout," *The Joslin Blog*, Joslin Diabetes Center, July 22, 2014. http://blog.joslin.org.

34. Hadley George, "Type One Teen Diabetes Burnout Survival Guide," Beyond Type 1, August 6, 2015. https://beyondtype1.org.

35. George, "Type One Teen Diabetes Burnout Survival Guide."

36. Lauren Stanford, "Why a Teen with Type 1 Diabetes Lied to Her Parents," ASweetLife, June 10, 2015. https://asweetlife.org.

37. Quoted in Diabetes UK, "Your Stories in Brief."

38. Quoted in Elizabeth Aguilera, "A Family's Struggles with Type 2 Diabetes," 89.3KPCC, September 22, 2016. www.scpr.org.

39. Quoted in Brink, "Type 2 Diabetes Surges in People Younger than 20."

40. Ortiz, "One Patient's Story."

41. Sarah Ball, "Teenager with Type 1 Diabetes," *The Diabetic Journey* (blog), August 3, 2017. https://thediabeticjourney .com.

42. Ball, "Teenager with Type 1 Diabetes."

Chapter 5: Can Diabetes Be Prevented?

43. Carla Greenbaum and Mark Harmel, "Preventing Type 1 Diabetes Before Symptoms Occur," Medscape, April 8, 2016. www.medscape.com.

44. Quoted in Yle Uutiset, "Finnish Diabetes Vaccine Trials to Start in 2018," July 19, 2017. https://yle.fi.

45. Jaakko Tuomilehto and Peter E.H. Schwarz, "Preventing Diabetes: Early Versus Late Preventive Interventions," *Diabetes Care*, August 2016, p. S118. http://care.diabetesjournals .org.

46. Centers for Disease Control and Prevention, "Prevent Type 2 Diabetes in Kids,"June 29, 2017. www.cdc.gov.

47. National Institute of Diabetes and Digestive and Kidney Diseases, "Preventing Type 2 Diabetes," November 2016. www .niddk.nih.gov.

48. Mary Kemp, "Standing Tall Amidst the Shame and Blame in Type 2 Diabetes," Diabetes Daily, October 13, 2015. www .diabetesdaily.com.

49. Kemp, "Standing Tall Amidst the Shame and Blame in Type 2 Diabetes."

American Diabetes Association (ADA)
2451 Crystal Dr., Suite 900
Arlington, VA 22202
website: www.diabetes.org

The ADA offers extensive information about every kind of diabetes, in both children and adults. The website link for Living with Diabetes leads to a special section on kids and type 2.

Children with Diabetes
8216 Princeton-Glendale Rd., PMB 200
West Chester, OH 45069
website: www.childrenwithdiabetes.com

This is an online community for kids with diabetes, their parents, their family members, and adults with diabetes. It offers discussion forums, educational articles, and the latest diabetes news.

Diabetes Canada
1400-522 University Ave.
Toronto, ON M5G 2R5
website: www.diabetes.ca

This organization offers information and support for all Canadians with diabetes or prediabetes and is working to reverse the diabetes epidemic. Online visitors can take a tour of Banting House, the home of Frederick Banting, known as "the birthplace of insulin." Information is also available about ongoing clinical trials, and a free diabetes information kit is available upon request.

Insulin Nation

website: http://insulinnation.com

People who use insulin are the "citizens" of this online community, which reports on the latest medical and scientific news for type 1 diabetes. Citizens contribute stories about living with diabetes, and the website supplies articles from around the world about diabetes research.

JDRF

26 Broadway, Fourteenth Floor
New York, NY 10004
website: www.jdrf.org

The JDRF (formerly known as the Juvenile Diabetes Research Foundation) is devoted to advocacy, research, and support for those with type 1 diabetes, whether children or adults. People with type 1 can find information, ask questions, join an online support group, or request free toolkits and guides to help them cope with their diabetes.

Joslin Diabetes Center

1 Joslin Pl.
Boston, MA 02215
website: www.joslin.org

Affiliated with Harvard University, the Joslin Diabetes Center is dedicated to conducting research to find a cure for diabetes and working to ensure that people with diabetes live long, healthy lives. At its website, visitors can find information about diabetes, news articles about the latest research, and a large, supportive online community.

For Further Research

Books

Emily Mahoney, *Diabetes: Diagnosis and Management*. Farmington Hills, MI: Lucent, 2018.

Patrick McAllister, *Highs & Lows of Type 1 Diabetes: The Ultimate Guide for Teens and Young Adults*. New York: Good Books, 2018.

Rebecca Sherman, *Diabetes and Other Endocrine Disorders*. Broomall, PA: Mason Crest, 2017.

Rae Simons, *A Kid's Guide to Diabetes*. Vestal, NY: Village Earth, 2016.

Jamie Wood and Anne Peters, *The Type 1 Diabetes Self-Care Manual*. Arlington, VA: American Diabetes Association, 2018.

Internet Sources

American Diabetes Association, "Safe at School." www.diabetes.org/living-with-diabetes/parents-and-kids/diabetes-care-at-school/?gclid=CjwKCAiA8bnUBRA-EiwAc0hZk9omGxl0sB4e0MHmW5ziNw_LtCAXWLERWXtlT3qudGb_Roe9kt26XRoCjOYQAvD_BwE.

American Heart Association, "Hey Kids, Learn About Blood Sugar and Diabetes," 2014. www.heart.org/HEARTORG/HealthyLiving /HealthyKids/LifesSimple7forKids/Hey-Kids-Learn-About-Blood -Sugar-and-Diabetes_UCM_466609_Article.jsp#.Wo8TANiW wdU.

Adam Brown, "10 Tips for Teenagers to Live Well with Type 1 Diabetes," diaTribe, July 27, 2015. https://diatribe.org/10-tips -teenagers-live-well-type-1-diabetes.

Insulin-Pumpers, "Meet the Kids Who Pump Insulin." www.insulin -pumpers.org/pkids.shtml.

KidsHealth, "Type 1 Diabetes: What Is It?" http://kidshealth.org /en/kids/type1.html.

Index

Cover: BananaStock/Thinkstock Images

7: E. Jason Wambsgans/MCT/Newscom

10: TheVisualMD/Science Source

13: Maury Aaseng

17: R. Kristoffersen/Shutterstock.com

24: parinyabinsuk/iStock/Thinkstock Images

27: dageldog/iStockphoto.com

29: Maury Aaseng

35: Garo/Phanie/Science Source

38: LightField Studios/Shutterstock.com

40: Francis Dean/DeanPictures/Newscom

44: Associated Press

49: Lezlie Sterling/ZUMA Press/Newscom

53: Solovyova/iStockphoto.com

57: Richard T. Nowitz/Science Source

61: jacoblund/iStockphoto.com

64: StockRocket/iStockphoto.com

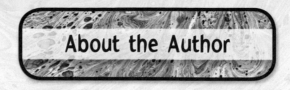

Toney Allman holds degrees from Ohio State University and the University of Hawaii. She currently lives in Virginia, where she enjoys a rural lifestyle as well as researching and writing about a variety of topics for students.